This is my favourite doll

This is
my house

My favourite
pop star is

....

My favourite animal is a ....

Now turn to the back of the book.

Printed and Published by D. C. Thomson & Co., Ltd.,
Dundee and London

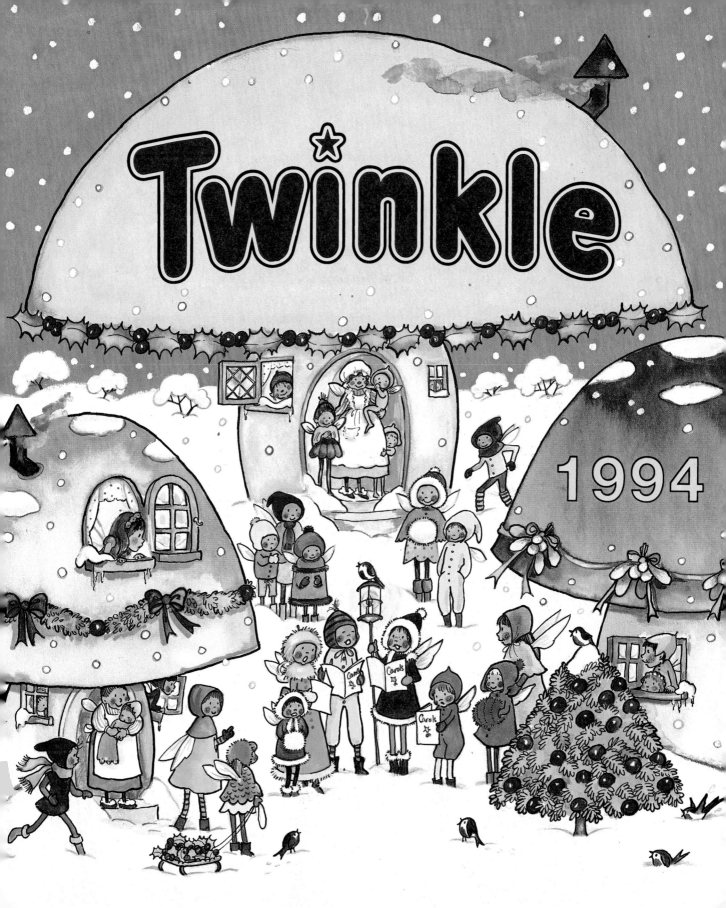

Dear, Girls,
  Hooray! It's **Twinkle Book** time again! I'm sure you'll enjoy this super book that's specially for you! **Fancy dress fun, Ellie Elephant, No more Christmas** and **The skating duck** are just some of the great stories you'll find inside.
  You'll have fun, too, with all your favourite **Twinkle** friends — **Nurse Nancy, Patch, Silly Milly, Penny Crayon, Ted and Zed, Fairy Fay** and lots more.
  There are also **puzzles to do** — and exciting **games to play!**
    Have fun!
      Love, *Twinkle*

Nurse Nancy

1 — It was Christmas Eve. Nancy, the little nurse at the Dollies Hospital, was making sure her patients were all comfortable before she went off duty.

2 — "I'm going carol-singing with three of my friends this evening," she told them. "You won't be alone, though. Grandad will be here to look after you."

3 — But just as Nancy was about to go off duty, the ambulance drew up with another patient. "I've got an accident victim!" called Colin the driver.

4 — The little nurse helped Colin to carry the patient indoors. "Will Belinda be all right?" asked Rosie, the doll's owner. "Her pram rolled away and she was thrown out."

5 — Mr Jingle, the dolly doctor, examined Belinda. "She needs emergency treatment," Grandad told Nancy. "I'm afraid you'll have to cancel your carol-singing."

6 — Nancy was disappointed, but she knew that Grandad couldn't mind the ward *and* fix Belinda. Nancy rang her three chums to tell them.

7 — Rosie waited anxiously for news of her dolly's condition. "Belinda will be fine now," said Nancy, tucking the bandaged dolly into bed. "She'll have to stay here for a few days."

8 — Later, when things had quietened down again, Nancy felt sad about missing the carol-singing. As she closed the curtains, the doorbell rang.

9 — "I hope it's not another emergency," she thought. When Nancy opened the door, however, she was surprised to find her chums there — dressed as nurses!

10 — "You couldn't come carol-singing with us, so we decided to sing with *you*!" laughed Sonya. Nancy *was* pleased. She wouldn't miss out, after all.

11 — All the patients joined in the nurses' carol concert. "Belinda won't mind staying in hospital now," smiled Rosie. "It's such a happy place. Merry Christmas, everyone!"

Patch

1 — One day, Paula Perkins' skating teacher took her class to the pond. Patch, Paula's kitten, went too.

2 — Patch enjoyed watching the skaters. He thought it looked like fun.

5 — Paula snuggled Patch close to her coat and went off round the ice. Patch thought it was super! Then the teacher said to Paula, "You've given me an idea. We'll do an ice show."

Can you see eight snowmen hidden on these pages?

3 — The little kitten decided to have a go, too. He carefully crept on to the ice. Luckily, Paula saw him and she scooped him up. "Oh, you silly kitten," she scolded.

4 — "You need *special* boots to skate. You can't do it on your own," she told him. Patch *did* look sad. "I know! I'll take you for a ride with me," she smiled. Patch purred happily.

6 — The following week, everyone was ready. The ice show was "Dick Whittington" with Paula playing the part of Dick, and Patch, of course, the cat!

LONDON

Winter fun-time

Find six whistles in the picture then colour it using your paints or crayons.

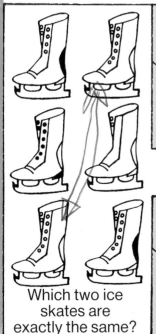

Which two ice skates are exactly the same?

Can you find six differences between these two pictures?

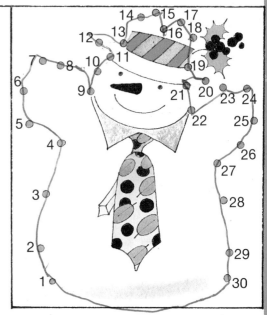

Join the dots to find a snowy friend.

Sam

SHONA MACGREGOR has a clever sheepdog called Sam. They live on a farm in the Scottish Highlands.

One day during the summer, Shona and Sam found an injured bird near the farm. It was a young ptarmigan and the gentle sheepdog carried it home.

"It looks very weak," sighed Shona. "I do hope we can save it."

Shona's mum helped make a bed for it in the henhouse. Every day, Shona visited the bird and, with food, rest and warmth, it began to grow bigger and stronger.

"If it continues to improve at this rate, we'll soon be able to release it into the wild again," Mrs MacGregor told Shona one day. "We'll use this basket to take it out to the moor when it's ready to leave."

Shona knew she'd be sorry to see the ptarmigan go but realised that it would be best for the young bird.

2 — There were lots of other things to keep Shona busy on the farm, and she liked to help Mr MacGregor as much as possible.

Even when the winter snows fell, the little girl enjoyed travelling all over the farm with him.

"Can we stop here and give Sam a run?" she asked after they had spent a busy morning taking bales of hay to cattle in far-off pastures.

"Of course," replied Mr MacGregor. "I could do with stretching my legs, too."

3 — While they were stopped, Sam became interested in the large, white birds flying overhead. He began gently barking at them, attracting Shona's attention.

"Why, these look just like the ptarmigan we've been looking after," she gasped. "But *they* can't be ptarmigan — they're *white*."

"They *are* ptarmigan," Mr MacGregor explained, "but they're in their winter plumage. They turn white so they can't be seen in the snow. That keeps them safe from their enemies."

He added that the ptarmigan was the only bird in this country that behaved in this way. In the winter, the bird's feathered feet even acted as snow shoes to help it cope with the snowy conditions.

But Shona was *still* puzzled.

"*Ours* hasn't changed colour," the little girl frowned. "Why is that?"

"Because we've kept him in a *heated* henhouse," chuckled Mr MacGregor. "He thinks it's still summer!"

4 — Shona was still smiling about that when they arrived back at the farm — but she soon stopped when she looked into the henhouse and discovered that the ptarmigan was no longer there!

"What can have happened to it?" she cried.

Then she noticed that the carrying basket beside its box had also vanished.

"Mummy must be going to set it free," Shona suddenly realised in horror. "But she mustn't, not yet. We'll have to wait until its feathers blend in with the countryside. It won't survive in snowy conditions when it still has its brown, summer coat."

But where had Mrs MacGregor taken it? That was the next problem.

Sam snuffled around the path outside, then, with a bark, trotted off down the road to the moor.

"There she is!" cried Shona a few minutes later. "Stop her, Sam!"

Sam raced off after her.

5 — Mrs MacGregor had knelt down and was just about to unfasten the catch on the carrying case when Sam bounded up to her.

The sheepdog jumped in between Shona's startled mummy and the case before she could let out the ptarmigan.

"Sam!" she yelled in surprise. "What *are* you playing at, you rascal? What a fright you gave me."

By then, Shona had arrived on the scene and was able to explain to Mrs MacGregor what a dreadful mistake she was about to make.

"It's a good job Sam *did* give me such a scare, then," she smiled. "We'd better take the ptarmigan back home and wait for a change in the weather."

And that's just what they did.

6 — It wasn't long before the snow melted away and spring arrived. As soon as Shona spotted the first brown ptarmigan, she and Sam set loose their fully-recovered patient.

"You'll be all right now," Shona called after it — and Sam barked *his* farewell, as if to say, "Safe journey!"

Polly

1 — Polly Penguin lives in Snowland. One day, Polly was going shopping. "It's cold today," she said. "I must wear my woolly scarf." But she couldn't find it!

2 — Soon, Polly passed Peter Polar Bear's house. "I need some shopping," he sighed, "but I can't find my woolly hat!" "Just come without it," smiled Polly.

3 — Later, in the shopping mall, they met Suki Seal. "What's wrong?" asked Polly. "My flippers are freezing," groaned Suki. "I couldn't find my woolly mitts!"

4 — In no time, the chums had finished shopping. "I have to pick Sue and Sally up from the park on the way home," said Suki. "We'll come with you," smiled Polly.

5 — The chums discovered that a snowman-building contest was taking place. "That's my scarf!" cried Polly. "And my hat!" shouted Peter.

6 — "I don't believe it!" squealed Suki. "I've just spotted my mitts." "Our things are all being worn by Sue and Sally's *snowman*!" chuckled Polly.

Binker

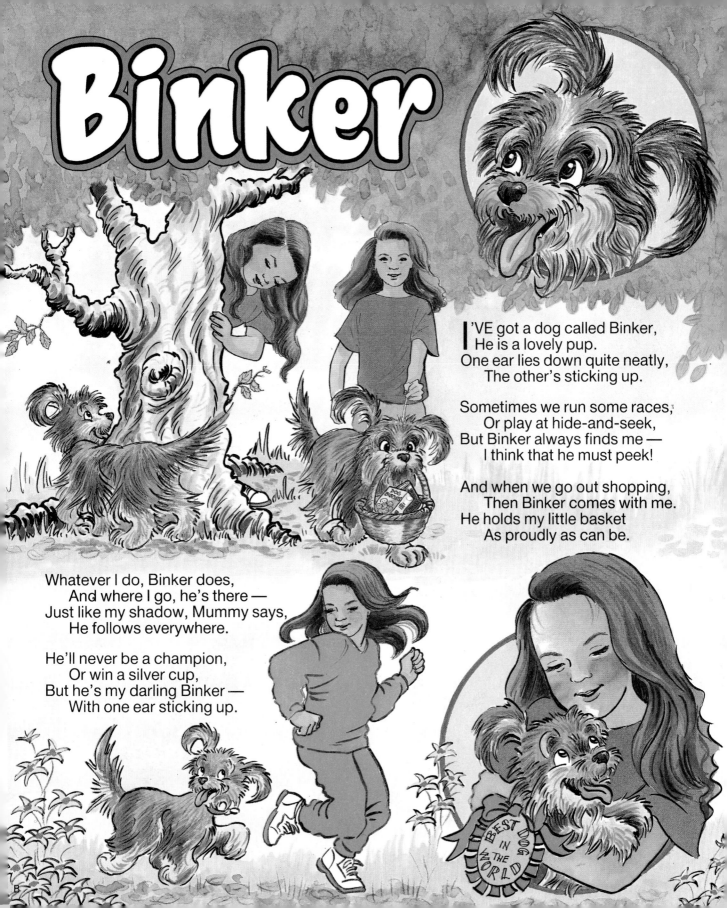

I'VE got a dog called Binker,
   He is a lovely pup.
One ear lies down quite neatly,
   The other's sticking up.

Sometimes we run some races,
   Or play at hide-and-seek,
But Binker always finds me —
   I think that he must peek!

And when we go out shopping,
   Then Binker comes with me.
He holds my little basket
   As proudly as can be.

Whatever I do, Binker does,
   And where I go, he's there —
Just like my shadow, Mummy says,
   He follows everywhere.

He'll never be a champion,
   Or win a silver cup,
But he's my darling Binker —
   With one ear sticking up.

Silly Milly

1 — Silly Milly is always in trouble. No matter what she does, it ends in a muddle. Very early on Christmas morning, Milly sneaked downstairs to open her presents.

2 — "Roller skates! I must try them out!" cheered our chum, dressing quickly. She couldn't skate very well and was soon out of control as she headed down a hill.

3 — Just in front of her, there was a hole in the pavement. Milly flew up a ramp and over the hole, but she collided with a bin on the other side.

4 — Our chum landed in a heap! The bin was sent flying, clattering noisily down the street. "What a racket!" gasped Milly. "I'd better chase after it and try to stop it."

5 — The little girl picked herself up and set off in pursuit of the rollaway bin. "I'm getting the hang of this now," she thought. But she couldn't stop when she wanted to.

6 — Milly *did* stop — when she landed in a hedge. "Help!" she shrieked. "What's going on?" called an angry man who'd been wakened by the noise.

7 — Our silly chum trekked home, only to find she was locked out. "No need to ask what you've been doing!" said Mum when she opened the door for her daughter.

8 — As Mum and Dad opened their presents after breakfast, they had to smile — Milly was fast asleep. "It'll be a peaceful Christmas this year!" chuckled Mum.

Fancy dress fun

1 — Rosie, Cherry and Holly Rabbit *always* dressed alike and no one could tell them apart. Once, their teacher scolded Cherry for getting all her sums wrong. But really it was Holly!

2 — Mummy always told off the wrong rabbit by mistake, too! "Holly, you greedy rabbit!" she called as Rosie ran off with a biscuit. And Rosie wouldn't say that she wasn't Holly!

3 — One day, the three rabbits were invited to Rupert Rabbit's fancy dress party. "Let's go as clowns," Holly suggested. But Mummy said if they all dressed the same, no one would win.

4 — So, on the day of the party, the sisters dressed differently. Rosie looked sweet as Little Bo-Peep, Holly was a cheeky clown and Cherry seemed very smart in her nurse's uniform.

5 — At the party, Rupert's daddy judged the fancy dress competition. To everyone's surprise, he presented first prize to Holly, second prize to Rosie and third prize to Cherry. They were thrilled to win!

6 — But on the way home, Holly gave Rosie her chocolate biscuits because they were her favourite, and Cherry gave Holly her calculator to help with her sums.

7 — Rosie gave Cherry the doll which had been her prize. "You can practise being a nurse and bandage her arms and legs," she suggested. So all the sisters were happy.

8 — Next day, the three rabbits appeared looking different. "We had such fun yesterday, we're going to be different *every* day," Holly explained. Now *everyone* was happy!

Cuddles and Co.

1 — Nadia *loved* animals and she had *lots* of pets. Among them were Cuddles the dog, Midge the cat, Tiny the kitten and Snowball the rabbit. But Nadia was bored.

2 — "I have *four* pets here to keep me company, but still I've no one to play with," she sighed. "They're too happy playing with each other."

3 — But soon, Cuddles noticed that Nadia was looking sad and the pets thought of a plan to cheer her up. "Here's what we should do," Cuddles woofed to the others.

4 — Nadia watched her pets rush round the garden as if they were looking for something. "What *are* they up to now?" she wondered as they collected things.

5 — She soon found out. Her pets were putting on a *circus* ! They did all sorts of clever tricks. Nadia clapped her hands and, before long, they had an audience.

6 — Now Nadia was no longer lonely. Everyone wanted *their* pets to join the animal circus. "My dog can sing," a girl called Carol told Nadia.

7 — There was an *amazing* number of talented pets. The juggling cat juggled, the singing dog sang and the performing poodle performed.

8 — Meanwhile, Snowball jumped over a balancing cat, Midge pushed a ball, and Tiny leapt on to a pot and Cuddles skateboarded through everyone. What a show!

CANDLE MAKER FOR A DAY!

Have you ever wondered how Christmas candles are made? Lori wrote to Twinkle to ask, so we decided to take her to Carberry Candles to find out.

1. At Carberry Candles, Lori discovered that candles can either be made in moulds or on the wick. Here's Lori with a mould.

2. Once the mould was fixed together, Lori poured in the wax. "This looks just like my mum's teapot," she giggled.

3. While the mould was setting, Lori had fun topping up a batch of scented candles.

4. Later, Lori met Anna, the candle painter. She gave Lori some tips on painting her cat candle.

5. Here is Lori with her finished cat candle. "I can't wait to show Mum and Dad," she beamed. Hasn't she made a lovely job?

6. Next, Lori looked at some fruity candles. "Mmm! This apple smells good enough to eat," she laughed.

7. Lori was surprised at how quickly white candles are coloured. "They just have to be dipped into coloured wax," she cried.

8. Carved candles are another of Carberry Candles' creations. First, the candles are dipped into lots of different-coloured wax and then cut and shaped into fancy designs.

9. Then it was Lori's turn. "Phew! This is hard work," she gasped. "You have to work really quickly before the wax cools."

10. Lori took a last look at the candles. "I've had a really nice time today," she smiled. "Thank you, Twinkle."

Special thanks to everyone at Carberry Candles.

Ellie Elephant

1 — Ellie Elephant loved music. One day, Ellie and her friend, Mary Mouse decided to join Miss Cat's animal band. Ellie was given a trumpet to play.

2 — But when she blew the trumpet, she blasted Fred Fox off his chair! "That elephant is a nuisance!" groaned the other musicians. Poor Ellie *was* disappointed!

3 — "Why don't you have a seat at the piano," suggested Miss Cat, the music teacher, "and I'll give you a lesson." Ellie headed for the keyboard.

4 — She plonked herself down on the stool. *Crash!* The legs broke and Ellie crashed to the floor! "I'm sorry," said Miss Cat, crossly. "I don't have anything suitable for you!"

5 — "Oh! I'll *never* be able to play in a band now," sighed Ellie. "Of course you will," smiled Mary. "We'll make up our own band. Let's go to the music shop!"

6 — "You'll need a strong instrument, Ellie," smiled Mary. "That big drum would be ideal!" "What will *you* play?" asked Ellie. "A little triangle like this," giggled the mouse.

7 — The following day, they performed in the park. "That's the best little band I've heard," chuckled Harry Hare. The crowd clapped and cheered. "More, more!" they cried. Ellie and Mary *were* delighted!

All you need to play is a dice and a counter for each player. Take turns to throw the dice, moving forward the number of places shown. Follow the instructions on the space you land on and the first player to reach the finish wins.

23 All your chums pile on to your sledge. Move on at high speed 4 spaces.

24

25 The sledge tips you off into a snowdrift. Go back 3 spaces.

26

27

22

21

28 A snowman is in your way but you dodge it. Go on 2 spaces.

20 A family of ducks holds you up. Go back 2 places.

29

19

30

31 You get lost in a snowstorm. Throw a 6 before going on.

18

32

FINISH

Nº 1

WEE Benny's sweet, but seldom neat,
    He's full of fun and joy.
He's grubby, friendly, naughty, cute,
    Like any little boy. He's . . .

My Baby Brother

"THE winter time is here again,"
    Sighed Ben, and sucked his thumb.
He sat and watched the wind and rain —
    He *did* look rather glum!

"But winter can be fun," I said.
    "No need to sit and frown."
In fact, that very afternoon,
    We caught the bus to town.

New lace-up boots for Ben, and then
    A jersey, red and thick,
A shiny football for his games,
    Just waiting for a kick!

Then we all had a special treat,
    Hot scones and cake for tea.
"Like summer's strawberries and cream!"
    Smiled Mum who winked at me.

And when November came around,
We made a super guy.
Ben clapped and cheered as rockets whizzed
And sparkled in the sky.

One day, I said, "It's Christmas soon!
We'll need some cards, you know."
We painted holly berries bright,
And robins in the snow.

On Christmas Eve, we carefully hung
Our stockings on the bed.
Ben even had a little sock —
Especially for Ted!

Then, what a jolly time we had
Around the Christmas tree.
"I think that winter's best of all!"
Young Benny called to me.

Penny Crayon

1 — Penny Crayon has *magic* crayons and her pictures come to life. Penny and her friend, Dennis, were on their way to a party.

2 — It was hard work trudging through the snow so Penny drew a sledge. "Jump on, Dennis," she cried.

3 — Dennis sat in front but, when the sledge came to a hill, it sped faster and faster downwards. "I can't steer!" wailed Dennis.

4 — "Don't worry," replied Penny. "How are we going to stop?" howled Dennis. "Hold on," answered Penny. But Dennis didn't.

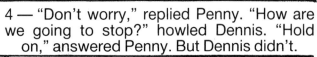

5 — Penny threw an anchor that she had drawn and she and the sledge stopped. But Dennis flew on and landed softly . . .

6 — . . . in a snowman! "Boo, hoo! My snowman's ruined," sobbed a little boy. Poor Dennis was snowbound.

7 — "I'll make you a *special* snowman," Penny promised the boy and he watched as she drew one which came to life! "Yippee!" cried the boy. "This snowman's really cool!"

8 — Then Penny gasped. "We'll be late!" Quickly, she drew a *flying* sledge — just like Santa's. Penny and Dennis reached the party after all!

Now use *your* crayons to colour this picture . . .

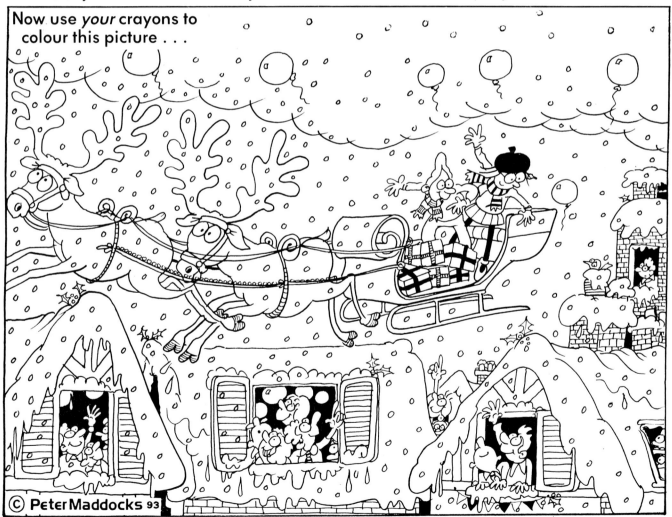

© Peter Maddocks 93

C

1 — Wendy Wilson has a most unusual friend, Winkle, a 300-year-old witch who lives in her attic! Winkle loves to help . . . even though not all her spells work as she plans!

2 — One day, Wendy had a problem. "My school teacher says we've to make up a story about being invisible," the little girl sighed, "but I don't know what to write."

3 — Winkle knew *just* what to do. She moved her wand and chanted, *"So you'll know just what to write — Wendy, vanish out of sight!"* And with that, Wendy became invisible!

4 — Only Winkle could see her chum — and when they went on the bus, Wendy found that being invisible might *not* be all fun. A fat girl *sat* on her! "I'm squashed!" she cried.

5 — By the time they reached the park, Wendy was feeling *most* put upon — not to mention sat upon. "Never mind," Winkle comforted her. "You'll have fun in here."

6 — However, when Wendy was on a roundabout, it whizzed round so fast she became dizzy. "Let me off!" Wendy wailed. But, of course, her chums couldn't see her.

7 — Next, her classmates organised a race. "This is more like it," beamed Wendy as she raced ahead of everyone to reach the tape first. But again, no one *saw* her win.

8 — "That's not fair," Wendy protested as her classmates chaired another girl as the winner. "*She* didn't win the race — I did. I might as well not be here."

9 — Even worse was to follow. One of the girls produced a bag of sweets but, when Wendy tried to take one, she was bowled over by the others, who didn't know she was there.

10 — "I've had enough of this," moaned Wendy. "I'm going home." At the bus stop, though, the bus drove past! "I *hate* being invisible," the little girl groaned.

11 — But when Wendy arrived home, it was past her bedtime — and at last she discovered that being invisible *did* have its uses. Mum didn't see her as she tiptoed to her room!

12 — Wendy's class essay got top marks. "It's as if you *know* what it's like to be invisible," smiled her teacher. "Thanks to Winkle, I *do* !" chuckled Wendy.

1 — Joni Jackson has a *most* unusual chum — Goopy, a goblin disguised as a cat! One day they spotted a poster . . .

2 — The chums set to work building their own model, but it looked *terrible.* "We'll never win with *that*," sighed Joni sadly.

3 — But Goopy used his powers and turned *himself* into a snowman. "Now we'll show 'em," he chuckled.

4 — But Bully Billy had spotted the super-duper snowman and rushed over to knock it down. "I'll make sure *you* don't win," he sneered.

5 — Of course, he didn't expect the snowman to fight back! "Ouch!" wailed Billy. "The snowman's *bitten* me!"

6 — "*He* won't interfere again," beamed Goopy. "Now let's get some clothes for me. A snowman's got to look his best!"

7 — Goopy saw what he needed outside a tailor's shop. "Just what the well-dressed snowman should wear!" he smiled.

8 — "Well, have you ever seen a smarter snowman?" the goblin asked. "You look real *cool*," laughed Joni.

9 — Just then, though, the tailor rushed up to them with a policeman following. "That's the snowman who stole my clothes!" he cried.

10 — Goopy gave back the clothes to the shopkeeper. "Now we've no chance of winning," sighed Joni.

11 — But crafty Goopy had one more flash of goblin inspiration . . .

12 — The chums *did* win the prize for the best snowman, because the judge had never seen a *technicolour* snowman before! "There's no one *quite* like Goopy," giggled Joni.

Ted and Zed

from Outer Space

1 — Ted, a space bear, and Zed, his faithful space dog, are visiting their friend, Susie, on Earth. "Let's ask Dad to take us to a wildlife park," the young girl suggested one day.

2 — On the way, though, Dad's car had a puncture. As he changed the wheel, the chums watched a queue form. "We'll never get to see the animals," sighed Susie.

3 — Sure enough, by the time Dad got the car on the road again, the traffic had slowed to a halt. "I know how we'll see the wildlife," grinned Ted, "but we'll have to go home."

4 — Susie *was* puzzled, till Ted told her to climb into his rocket, which was parked in the garden. "We'll be back in time for tea," the space bear called to Dad.

5 — "But where are we going?" asked Susie as the rocket *zoomed* off. "Haven't you guessed?" chuckled Ted. "We're going to see wildlife — but not in a park . . ."

6 — Ted steered the rocket through the skies till finally he cried, "We're almost there! Get your camera ready, Susie. You'll soon see all the animals you could possibly want!"

7 — Susie could hardly believe her eyes as Ted's rocket flew over *Africa.* "We'll just be in time for the chimps' tea party," chuckled Ted. "Everyone will be there."

8 — When the chums arrived home, it was time for *their* tea. "Aren't you hungry?" asked Mum. "Not really," giggled Susie. "We've had tea already," explained Ted and Zed.

9 — Then Susie showed her photos. "And I thought you'd be *disappointed* at missing the wildlife park," gasped Dad. "Life's never dull with Ted and Zed!" chuckled Susie.

Polly's Puzzle Time

Emma Eskimo is having a Christmas party. Can you lead Polly Penguin and her chums through the maze to Emma's igloo?

Polly and her chums have taken lots of Christmas presents for Emma. Which two are exactly the same?

The chums are all wearing the wrong party hats. Rearrange the letters on the hats and then match them to their owner.

Find six Christmas crackers hidden in the picture above, then colour it using your paints or crayons.

Buzzy

Buzzy's helping at a Christmas jumble sale.

Everyone wanted to buy *something* . . .

. . . except a single sock.

Buzzy had a use for it, though.

She used it for *her* Christmas stocking!

Happy Birthday

1 — Katie *was* upset when she saw it was snowing. "It's my birthday but none of my friends will get here now," she wailed.

2 — She was even sadder when Mum and Dad gave her their present. "It's too small to be what I wanted," she sighed.

To find the gift we have for you, You'll have to hunt the whole house through. So off you go, don't feel blue— Maybe the shower will give you a clue!

3 — But Katie got a surprise when she opened the box. Inside, there was a note.

4 — "It's a treasure hunt!" Katie shouted gleefully. "All I have to do is follow the clues and they'll lead me to my proper present! This is going to be a fun birthday after all!"

One clue done, three more to go— For the next you'll need to know Where your father keeps the hoe. The answer's high instead of low.

5 — Katie raced into the bathroom and found the next clue on the shower curtain.

6 — "All Daddy's tools are in the garage," cried Katie. "That's where the next clue will be. Oh, I *am* enjoying this!" And off the little girl set once again.

7 — Sure enough, there, tied to the top of the hoe, was Katie's next clue. "What does *this* one say?" she giggled excitedly.

8 — She remembered that Mummy's pile of ironing had been blocking the door of her toy cupboard. "I know!" she yelled.

9 — Katie rushed to the airing cupboard. In it she found the ironing — *and* the final clue!

10 — "So it was in here all the time," she laughed. But though Katie searched high and low, under the chairs and under the table, she couldn't find her present.

11 — "Maybe I'll find it after tea," she sighed, lifting the tea cloth.

12 — There was her present — the model farm she wanted! "I hope the snow hasn't spoiled your birthday," said Daddy. "Oh, no!" beamed Katie. "It's made it the best one *ever*!"

Fairy Fay

1 — It was Christmas Eve, and Fairy Fay and her chums were setting the table in the Fairyland Hall. They were holding a special tea-party for the Fairy Queen.

2 — There was lots of delicious food including a big, wobbly jelly. "Everything looks splendid," Fay remarked. "Now let's fetch the chairs."

FUN FAIR
Closed
until Spring
SAMMY SPRITE
(Proprietor)

3 — The Fairyland folk were in for a shock, however. The chairs were torn and broken. "We can't put *these* out," sighed Eddie Elf. "They're not fit for the queen to sit on."

4 — "We must do something!" gasped the others. Well, nobody knew what to do, until Fay sprang into action. "I'll ask Sammy Sprite to help us," she said.

5 — Sammy ran the funfair. Fay told him about the broken chairs. "I'm sorry, I don't have any to spare," Sammy told her. "But you can still help out," smiled Fay.

6 — "I don't want to borrow your chairs," she added. Fay led him to one of the rides in the funfair. "I'd like to borrow *these*," she said, pointing to the giant teacups.

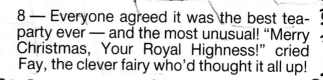

7 — The Fairy Queen was surprised when she entered the Fairyland Hall. "What a perfect setting for a tea-party!" she exclaimed, sitting in one of the cups.

8 — Everyone agreed it was the best tea-party ever — and the most unusual! "Merry Christmas, Your Royal Highness!" cried Fay, the clever fairy who'd thought it all up!

A picture to Colour

Before you colour this picture, count the number of cats. Then see if you can find six hidden bowls.

"No more Christmas!"

SUZY and Sammy Seal popped their heads up through the ice and heard voices.

"It's the Ice Queen," whispered Suzy.

"Listen!" whispered Sammy.

"You will capture Santa Claus on Christmas Eve," said the Ice Queen. "You will throw all the presents into the sea and keep Santa and his reindeer locked up until Christmas is over."

"Yes, Your Majesty," answered a troop of King Penguins at once.

They were the Ice Queen's servants.

"No more Christmas!" said the Ice Queen. "I *hate* Christmas!"

2 — Suzy and Sammy were horrified.

"We must get help!" gasped Suzy.

The seals ran to Percy Polar Bear's cave where they found some friends.

3 — "The Ice Queen's planning to hijack Santa Claus!" cried Sammy.

"What?" roared Percy.

"It's true!" sobbed Suzy. "We heard her order her servants to capture Santa."

"She must not get away with this!" said Wilbert Walrus.

"But what can we do?" asked Christopher Caribou, shaking his antlers in despair. "There isn't time to send a message to the North Pole to warn Santa."

"*We* could ride past, pretending to be Santa's sleigh," said Archie Arctic Fox.

"But how?" asked Sammy.

"We'll get a sledge," explained Archie. "Percy can dress up as Santa, and Christopher can be a reindeer. The rest of us will pretend to be parcels!"

5 — But, instead of stopping, Christopher and his friend pulled the sleigh faster and faster down the hill. The Ice Queen and her servants gave chase. Carefully, Percy guided the sleigh over a frozen river and stopped on the other side.

Suddenly, the Ice Queen stopped.

"I hear sleigh bells!" she exclaimed.

And there, at the top of a hill, was the *real* Santa Claus!

"Ho! Ho! Ho! Fooled you!" chuckled Percy.

4 — On Christmas Eve, they were ready and they set off on their journey. As they passed the Ice Queen's palace, a cry of "Halt!" rang out.

6 — The Ice Queen was furious! She shook her fist and stamped her foot. She stamped so hard the ice cracked! Before the Ice Queen could escape, she and all her servants fell through into the freezing water.

"Ho, ho, ho! That will teach you," scoffed Percy.

Santa went safely on his way, unaware of the Ice Queen's wicked plot. And, once again, boys and girls all over the world had a lovely Christmas!

D

Cinderella Puzzle Story

Cinderella lived with her wicked stepmother and two ugly sisters. They were very cruel and made Cinderella do all the housework.

Every morning, Cinderella had to clean the old cinders from the fireplace. Soon she became known as Cinders.

Can you find six differences between these two pictures?

One day, Cinderella was sad because she wasn't allowed to go to a grand ball at the palace. All of a sudden, there was a flash of light and a strange lady appeared.

Y I   T O R H G
R F A   E O M D

Rearrange the letters to find who she was.

The lady told her to fetch six mice, two birds and a pumpkin.
Which two mice are exactly the same?

When she waved her wand, the pumpkin turned into a coach, the mice into horses and the birds into footmen! Then she waved the wand over Cinderella and her ragged dress became a beautiful ball gown. On her feet were dainty glass slippers. "You must be home by midnight," the lady warned.
Lead the coach through the maze to the palace.

The answer to the jumbled letters puzzle is FAIRY GODMOTHER

Cinderella was very nervous when she arrived at the palace. Everyone in the ballroom gasped as they had never seen anyone so beautiful.

Then there was another gasp as the king's son, Prince Charming, stepped forward and asked Cinderella to dance with him.

Find the ugly sisters then colour the picture.

Cinderella had such a lovely time at the ball that she forgot all about the time and the Fairy Godmother's warning! When the clock struck twelve, Cinderella rushed out of the ballroom.
Draw the hands on the clock at the right time, then join the dots to see what Cinderella lost.

The next day, Prince Charming ordered all the ladies to try on the glass slipper. The stepsisters were surprised when the slipper fitted Cinderella. Prince Charming and Cinderella were soon married and lived happily ever after.
Find six rings and six birds in this picture.

Elfie

1 — Elfie is a little elf who lives in Mary's doll's house. The little girl doesn't know he's there, and when he makes things happen, Mary believes there's magic at work!

2 — One day, Elfie watched as Mary made patch pictures of a pierette and a harlequin. "I'd love a pierette costume to wear at the fancy dress party," Elfie heard her sigh.

3 — No one was more surprised than Mary when her mummy gave her a surprise — a pierette costume! "Oh, thank you!" she cried. "Now I hope I meet a harlequin."

4 — Elfie liked parties, too, so as soon as Mary had left, he shouted to his friends, the mice. "We'll have a party as well," he called excitedly. "Come dressed up!"

5 — The little elf wasn't looking where he was running, though, and he crashed into the pot of paste Mary had been using for her pictures. "What a mess!" he wailed.

6 — But Elfie knew how to make the best of his problem. He began to fix Mary's paper squares on to his sticky clothes. "I'll make myself into a harlequin," he grinned.

7 — Soon the costume was finished — and what fun Elfie and his friends had at their party. They played lots of games and everyone admired Elfie's new suit.

8 — There was *another* surprise awaiting Mary. Elfie had put the costume on a doll. "There was no harlequin at my party — but *here's* one!" she gasped. "It's magic!"

Mix 'n' Match

Up to four people can play this game. First, make 24 cards by cutting up
each of the figures along the dotted lines as shown. Shuffle the cards
then lay them face down on a table. Throw a dice to see who plays first.
Then take turns to pick a card. If you turn over a card with a number you
already hold you must replace it. First player to make a figure is the winner.

Tina's magic toybox

1 — The day after Christmas, Tina was looking at her presents. One of them was a super magic set.

2 —"I'll play with this later," she thought, putting it into her magic toybox. "Tina — Lucy's here!" called Mummy from downstairs.

3 — Lucy was having a party later, but she didn't look happy. "The magician is ill," she sighed.

4 — "Never mind," Tina consoled her. "I'm sure we'll enjoy ourselves anyway." As Tina dressed for the party, her magic toybox opened and out popped a magician!

5 — He had come to life from the box of Tina's magic set! "Please perform at Lucy's party," asked Tina. "My pleasure," he smiled.

6 — His act was fantastic. Lucy was having such fun she forgot to ask where Tina had found Mr Trix — which was probably just as well!

The skating duck!

THE ducks who lived on the little island in the middle of the village pond looked out for Helen and her grandad coming to feed them every day.

2 — "Quack! Quack!" cried one duck, meaning, "Here they come!"

And, as if the cry had been a starter's whistle, the ducks dived into the water. *Splash! Splash! Splash!*

"Oh, look, Grandad! They're having a race towards us!" cried Helen.

The ducks in the lead easily reached the crumbs and gobbled them up hungrily. But one little duck that Helen had named "Daisy", lagged way behind. She was *always* last.

By the time she reached Helen and Grandad, there were no crumbs left.

"Oh, you poor thing," sighed Helen. "You'll have to learn to go faster."

3 — Next day, Grandad told Helen to take her skates to the pond.

"I passed the pond this morning," he said. "The water is frozen and safe enough for skating on."

Helen *loved* skating and it was fun to skate on the pond. It was bumpy and rough, not flat and smooth like the ice rink. And everyone was skating in different directions instead of the one-way system at the ice rink. Helen giggled as she just missed a boy who tripped towards her.

4 — "This is great fun, Grandad! Can we stay longer?" Helen asked.

When Grandad nodded, "Yes," Helen skated over towards the island. She noticed Daisy gingerly stepping on to the ice.

Whoops! Daisy skidded all over the place! The little duck staggered to her feet, and promptly slipped down again!

Helen chuckled at the duck's funny antics.

5 — As Helen skated closer, Daisy stopped and watched her as if trying to learn from her! Then the little duck made her way, waddling and skidding, towards Helen, as if she was trying to copy Helen's skating movements!

"You're trying to *skate,*" laughed Helen, and she tried to teach the duck to glide over the ice. "That's right," the little girl coaxed. "Use your wings to help you balance."

6 — Soon it was time for Helen and Grandad to go home for lunch. They didn't forget the ducks, however, and returned that afternoon with crumbs for them. The ducks on the island popped up as if to say, "Feeding Time!" Then they made their way to the edge of the island ready to race towards Helen and Grandad with their crumbs.

"Ready, steady, go!" cried Helen. "Here they come!"

"I suppose poor Daisy will be last again," sighed Grandad.

7 — But, to Helen and Grandad's surprise, Daisy began to 'skate' over the icy pond and she took the lead while the other ducks floundered and fell.

"*Quack! Squawk! Screech!*" they cried as they slipped and slid.

"Good girl, Daisy!" cheered Helen while Grandad gasped in surprise.

8 — In no time at all, Daisy reached the crumbs.

"How did Daisy manage that?" asked Grandad.

"*I* taught her to *skate*!" exclaimed Helen.

"Well, you've both done very well," chuckled Grandad.

And with a *quackety-quack,* Daisy agreed.

SAFE FOR SKATING

My favourite sport is .... *ice skating*

Fill in this picture with all your favourite colours.

On holiday I like to ....

My favourite toy is my

....